The Rieding Violin Concerto in B Minor

Practice Edition

A Learn Violin Practically Book

Concerto, Op. 35 by Oskar Rieding
Written and Compiled by Cassia Harvey
Duet by Myanna Harvey, based on Oskar Rieding

CHP365

©2020 C. Harvey Publications   All Rights Reserved.

www.charveypublications.com - print books
www.learnstrings.com - downloadable books
www.harveystringarrangements.com - chamber music

Table of Contents

Section	Page
What's In the Book	3
How to Practice Using This Edition	4
Understanding Symbols and Terms	5
Reading and Playing Half and Whole Steps	6
Finger Patterns Used in Rieding	6
Playing Staccato and Using it to Help Rhythm	8
What to Focus on in Each Movement	9
Welcome!	10
Movement One - Preparatory Exercises	11
Movement One - With Study Notes	22
Movement Two - Preparatory Exercises	26
Movement Two - With Study Notes	30
Movement Three - Preparatory Exercises	32
Movement Three - With Study Notes	42
Concerto in B Minor - Complete Piece	
Movement One	46
Movement Two	48
Movement Three	50
Concerto in B Minor - Violin Duet	
Movement One	54
Movement Two	59
Movement Three	62
Concerto (Violin II Part for Performance)	68
Concerto in B Minor - Piano Accompaniment	
Movement One	75
Movement Two	80
Movement Three	83
Violin Curriculum Segments - Where to Place Rieding	89

What's In the Book

How to Practice Using This Edition
These pages have ideas for developing a practice strategy to learn the Concerto. From explanations of symbols and terms to a description of half and whole steps, these pages tell you how the book can be most helpful to you.

Preparatory Exercises
The most difficult parts in the Concerto were identified and then broken down and taught in these pages. The Preparatory Exercises for each movement are followed by the "Movement with Study Notes."

Movements With Study Notes
Each movement of the Concerto is written with notes for study, including high and low finger marks, some beat marks, another reminders.

Complete Concerto
The entire violin part to the Concerto is here, for practice or performance.

Concerto with Violin Duet Part
The entire Concerto is included with a violin duet part that will allow you to practice or perform the piece with your teacher or with another violinist. If you'd like to perform the duet, the Violin II part is included by itself, after the score, so page turns can be easier.

Piano Accompaniment
The piano accompaniment is included for study, practice, or performance.

Violin Curriculum Segment - Where to Place the Rieding Concerto
These pages show how the Rieding Concerto in B minor can fit in a violin curriculum, along with recommended methods, etudes, and supplemental study books.

©2020 C. Harvey Publications   All Rights Reserved.

How to Practice Using This Edition

1. Play and master the **Preparatory Exercises** for each movement.

2. You may also, at the same time, practice the piece using the **Movement with Study Notes** that follows each set of Preparatory Exercises.

3. Once you have learned the movement fairly well, transition to the same movement (without study notes) in the **Complete Piece** section (pages 46-53.)

4. The entire book can be played with free **Play-Along** files. See below for more information.

5. Play the **Concerto with Duet** part with your teacher or with another violinist.

6. If you know a pianist, play the Concerto with the included **Piano Accompaniment**.

7. See what to play next in a typical violin curriculum, using the lists at the end of the book.

Play-Along Sound Files

Play-Along Sound Files for this book can be found at https://soundcloud.com/charveypublications/sets/riedingviolinbminor.

The files are listed according to their page in the book.

Soundcloud can be accessed on your computer or on your mobile device, via their free app.

©2020 C. Harvey Publications All Rights Reserved.

Understanding Symbols and Terms

Rhythm is taught by the addition of small notes above the regular notes that indicate how you might subdivide the notes you are playing. They often, but not always, indicate what the piano is playing.

Metronome markings are included in the Movements with Study Notes for both study and performance tempos. They are listed as a range (i.e. from 60-84). When you have learned the notes and bowings fairly well, you might want to start playing with the metronome and you can start the first movement at a quarter note = 60. As you progress, move the metronome up one or two notches and keep practicing. Continue getting faster until you reach the performance tempo where you feel most comfortable.

These markings are only approximate; feel free to play the piece at a slower or faster tempo!

Arrows are sometimes used to indicate when a finger needs to be lower or higher.

In this case, move the 2nd finger back to "low" position (a half step away from 1st finger.)

In this example, move the 1st finger up to "high" position (a half step away from 2nd finger.)

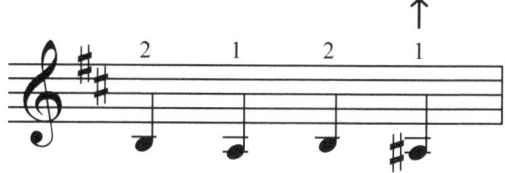

©2020 C. Harvey Publications All Rights Reserved.

Reading and Playing Half Steps

Here are some practical ways to think of steps on the violin:

• When two fingers are next to each other with little or no space between them, you have reached a half step.

• When there is space for one extra finger between your two fingers, you have reached a whole step.

In this book, **half steps** are marked this way:

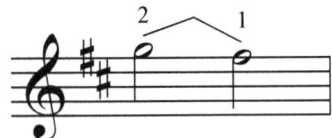

Please note: If a half step mark is indicated across two strings, it refers to the half-step (close) space between the fingers, even though the two notes are not a half step apart in music.

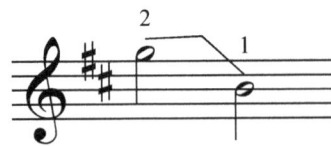

Finger Patterns Used in the First Movement

©2020 C. Harvey Publications All Rights Reserved.

Finger Patterns Used in the Second Movement

Finger Patterns Used in the Third Movement

©2020 C. Harvey Publications All Rights Reserved.

Playing Staccato and Using it to Help Rhythm

- Staccato is played by stopping your bow sharply on the string.

- In this book, several staccato notes in one bow are used to teach rhythm.

- While the bow is moving in the same direction, stop the bow completely on the string to make each note with an articulation dot on top.

- The bow should make a short, sharp sound for each note.

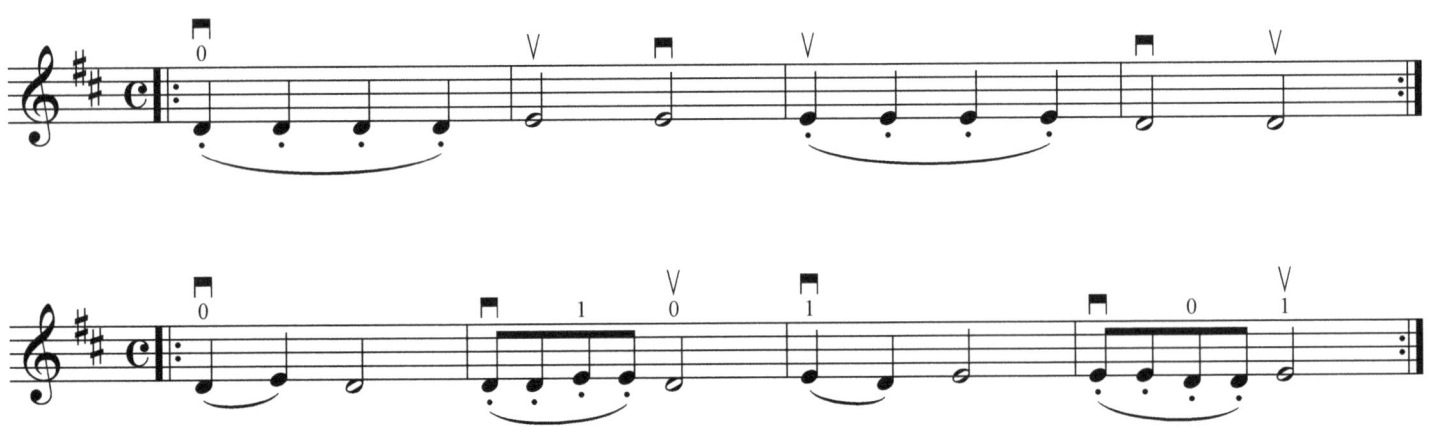

There are 3 eighth notes inside a dotted quarter note.
Use staccato in measure 3 to help yourself hear the rhythm in measure 4.

©2020 C. Harvey Publications All Rights Reserved.

What to Focus on in Movement One

- Play with long bows and a bold, strong tone.

- Make sure each finger stops the string completely; this will give you the clearest sound.

- Focus on rhythm and counting correctly. Count the dotted quarter notes in this movement carefully by sub-dividing into eighth notes.

- You may want to first play without slurs, at a slow tempo, and then incorporate the printed bowings when you are ready to play faster.

What to Focus on in Movement Two

- Count carefully. In 6/8 timing, the following note values are observed:

    ♪ = 1 beat   ♩ = 2 beats   ♩. = 2 beats   𝅘𝅥𝅯 = 1/2 beat   𝅗𝅥. = 6 beats

    ♪♪ = ♩ = 1 beat   ♩.♪ = 4 beats

- If you are learning vibrato, use the ♩ and ♩. and ♩.♪ notes to practice a wide vibrato.

What to Focus on in Movement Three

- Focus on bringing out the drama in this movement. Take note of the contrast between the more exciting and more lyrical sections.
- Follow the dynamics carefully to make the music as dramatic as possible.

©2020 C. Harvey Publications All Rights Reserved.

Welcome!

Thank you for your purchase!

If you are happy with the book or have helpful information about it for other musicians and teachers, it would be super helpful if you could leave a review where you bought the book!

If you have a question about anything in this book, if there is anything you don't understand, or if there is anything you disagree with and you want to let us know, please reach out to us at charveypublications@gmail.com; we're happy to address your issue!

If there is any defect with the printed book, please know that we ourselves do not print the books. The best way to resolve a book printing issue is to contact the company where you purchased this book (or contact us if you purchased from www.charveypublications.com) for a full refund or exchange. If you discover a defect after the return window has closed, please notify the company so they can make appropriate changes at their printing facility and then contact us at charveypublications@gmail.com so we can help you to get a correctly printed copy of the book you can use.

Above all, we want your playing and teaching experience to be better because of our books. Suggestions, ideas, criticisms and positive comments are always welcome at charveypublications@gmail.com.

We realize that paperback binding is not ideal for sheet music, however it allows us to offer this, and all of our other books, for less than half as much as we would have to charge for different binding. If you'd like a downloadable copy of this book to play from a tablet or to print out, visit www.learnstrings.com and use code **printbookrieding** to get 30% off your purchase of a PDF copy.

And visit us at https://www.charveypublications.com/better-string-playing-blog for free sheet music that you might find helpful!

Here's to better string playing!

Cassia Harvey

©2020 C. Harvey Publications   All Rights Reserved.

The Rieding Violin Concerto in B Minor - Preparatory Exercises for Movement One

11

©2020 C. Harvey Publications All Rights Reserved.

The Rieding Violin Concerto in B Minor - Preparatory Exercises for Movement One

5. Rhythm Duet
Measures 8-12

©2020 C. Harvey Publications   All Rights Reserved.

6. Finger Agility Across Strings: Measures 16-20

7. Finger Exercise and Bowing Study: Measures 21-27

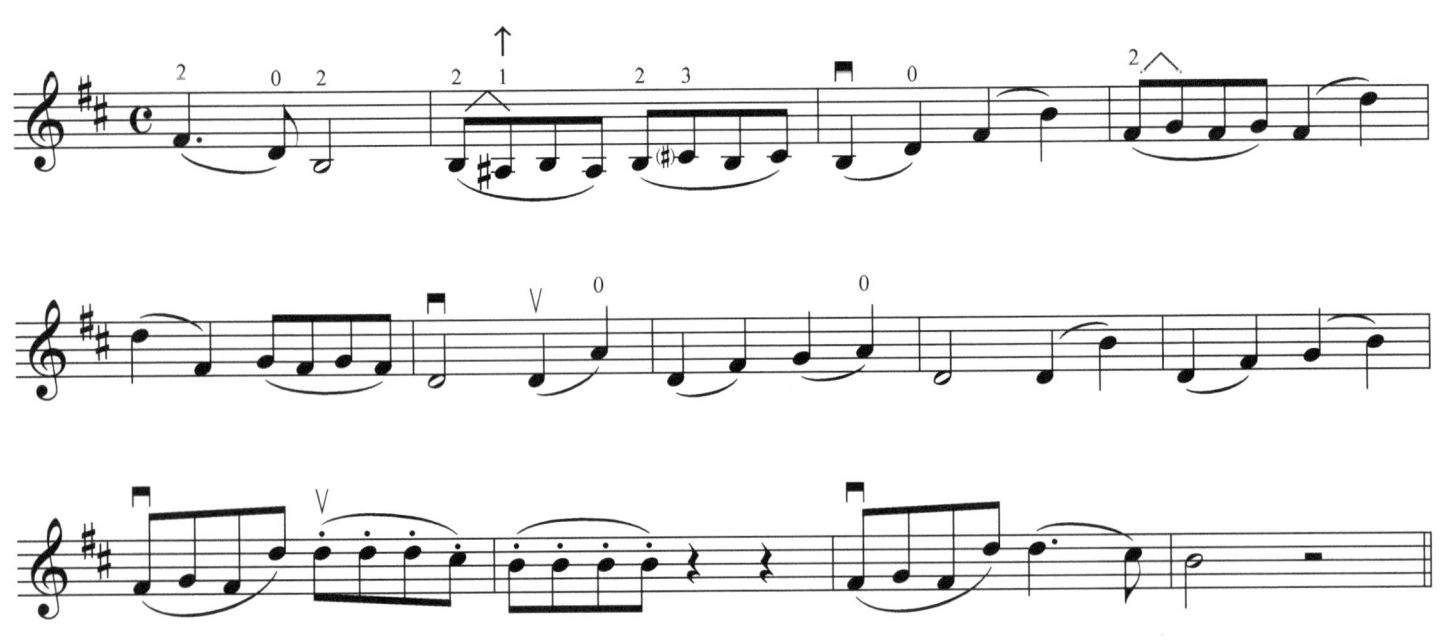

©2020 C. Harvey Publications   All Rights Reserved.

The Rieding Violin Concerto in B Minor - Preparatory Exercises for Movement One

15

8. Learning the Notes
Measures 26-28

9. High and Low Third Finger
Measures 29-32

©2020 C. Harvey Publications All Rights Reserved.

The Rieding Violin Concerto in B Minor - Preparatory Exercises for Movement One

10. Little Scales and Arpeggios: Measures 41-42

11. Learning the Notes: Measures 43-44

©2020 C. Harvey Publications All Rights Reserved.

The Rieding Violin Concerto in B Minor - Preparatory Exercises for Movement One

©2020 C. Harvey Publications   All Rights Reserved.

The Rieding Violin Concerto in B Minor - Preparatory Exercises for Movement One

16. Bowing: Measures 44-51

17. Finger Positions on One String: Measures 44-53

18. Low and High Second Finger: Measures 58-59

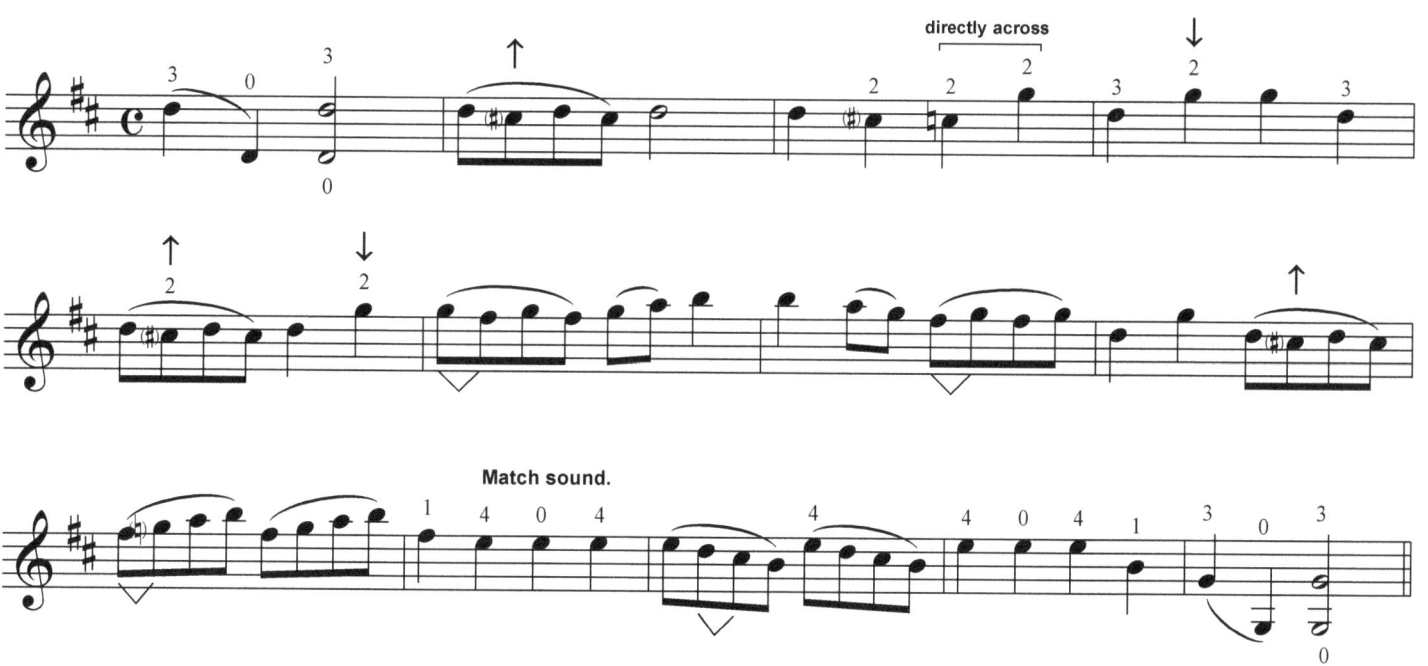

©2020 C. Harvey Publications All Rights Reserved.

20

The Rieding Violin Concerto in B Minor - Preparatory Exercises for Movement One

19. Finger Patterns:

20. Bowing: Measures 73-76

©2020 C. Harvey Publications   All Rights Reserved.

The Rieding Violin Concerto in B Minor - Preparatory Exercises for Movement One

21. Crossing to High First Finger: Measures 76-80

22. Crossing to High First Finger Review: Measures 8-9, 66-67

©2020 C. Harvey Publications All Rights Reserved.

Movement One With Study Notes

O. Rieding
Edited by C. Harvey

Allegro Moderato: Moderately (medium) lively or quick.

Study Tempo: ♩=60-84   Performance Tempo: ♩=84-112

©2020 C. Harvey Publications All Rights Reserved.

The Rieding Violin Concerto in B Minor - Movement One With Study Notes

24 — The Rieding Violin Concerto in B Minor - Movement One With Study Notes

©2020 C. Harvey Publications   All Rights Reserved.

This page is left blank for page turns.

©2020 C. Harvey Publications   All Rights Reserved.

The Rieding Violin Concerto in B Minor - Preparatory Exercises for Movement Two

1. Learning the Spaces and Playing in Tune
Measures 5-10

2. Rhythm
Measures 5-12

©2020 C. Harvey Publications   All Rights Reserved.

The Rieding Violin Concerto in B Minor - Preparatory Exercises for Movement Two

3. High and Regular Third Finger
Measures 19-20

4. New Finger Spacing with Flats
Measures 21-31

©2020 C. Harvey Publications All Rights Reserved.

The Rieding Violin Concerto in B Minor - Preparatory Exercises for Movement Two

5. Finger Spacing in 6/8 Timing: Measures 21-31

6. Little Arpeggios: Measures 21-31

**First play this exercise without slurs.
Then, add the slurs and play again.**

©2020 C. Harvey Publications   All Rights Reserved.

The Rieding Violin Concerto in B Minor - Preparatory Exercises for Movement Two

Movement Two With Study Notes

O. Rieding
Edited by C. Harvey

Andante: At a moderately slow "walking" tempo

Study Tempo: ♪=84-104 Performance Tempo: ♪=108-132

The Rieding Violin Concerto in B Minor - Movement Two With Study Notes

©2020 C. Harvey Publications   All Rights Reserved.

The Rieding Violin Concerto in B Minor - Preparatory Exercises for Movement Three

The Rieding Violin Concerto in B Minor - Preparatory Exercises for Movement Three

For work on m. 12, see Exercises 10-12.

5. Finger Agility I: Measures 19-20

6. Finger Agility II: Measures 23-24

©2020 C. Harvey Publications   All Rights Reserved.

The Rieding Violin Concerto in B Minor - Preparatory Exercises for Movement Three

7. Rhythm Duet
Measures 21-27

©2020 C. Harvey Publications All Rights Reserved.

The Rieding Violin Concerto in B Minor - Preparatory Exercises for Movement Three

10. Slurs Patterns and Staccato: Measures 12, 50

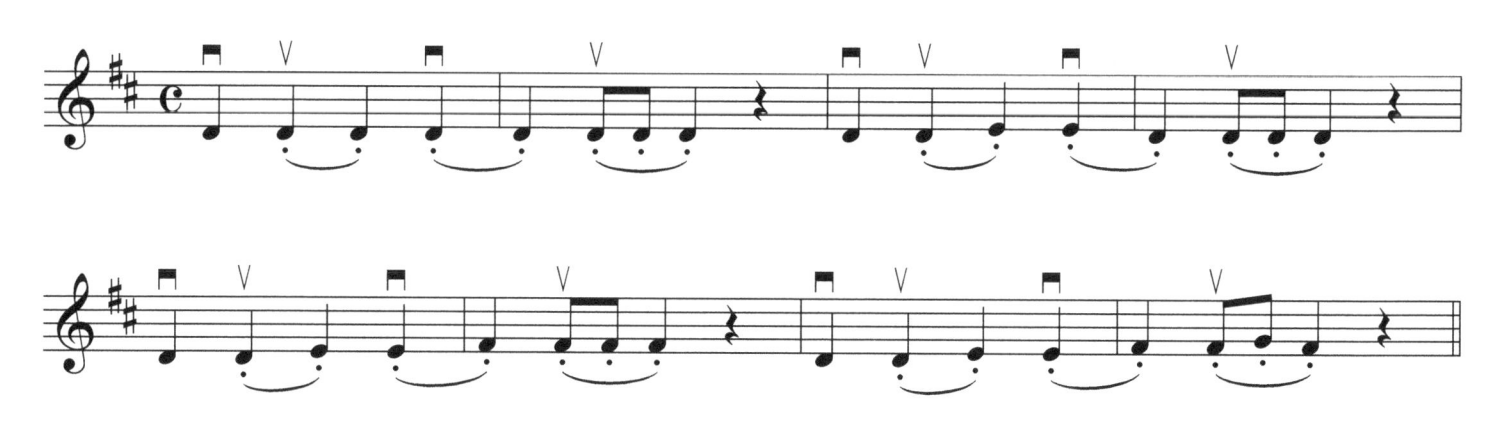

11. Changing Fingers Inside the Slurs: Measures 12, 50

Play this section four times.

12. Learning the Slurs: Measures 12, 50

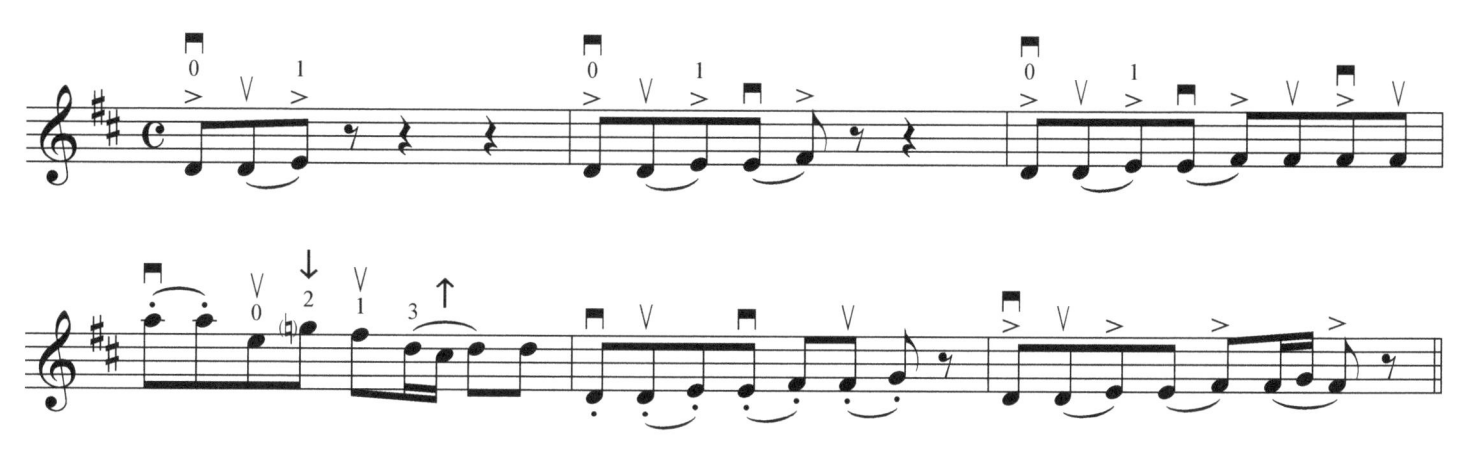

©2020 C. Harvey Publications   All Rights Reserved.

The Rieding Violin Concerto in B Minor - Preparatory Exercises for Movement Three

13. Finger Spacing and Rhythm: Measures 57-72

14. Crossing Strings Rhythmically: Measures 73, 75

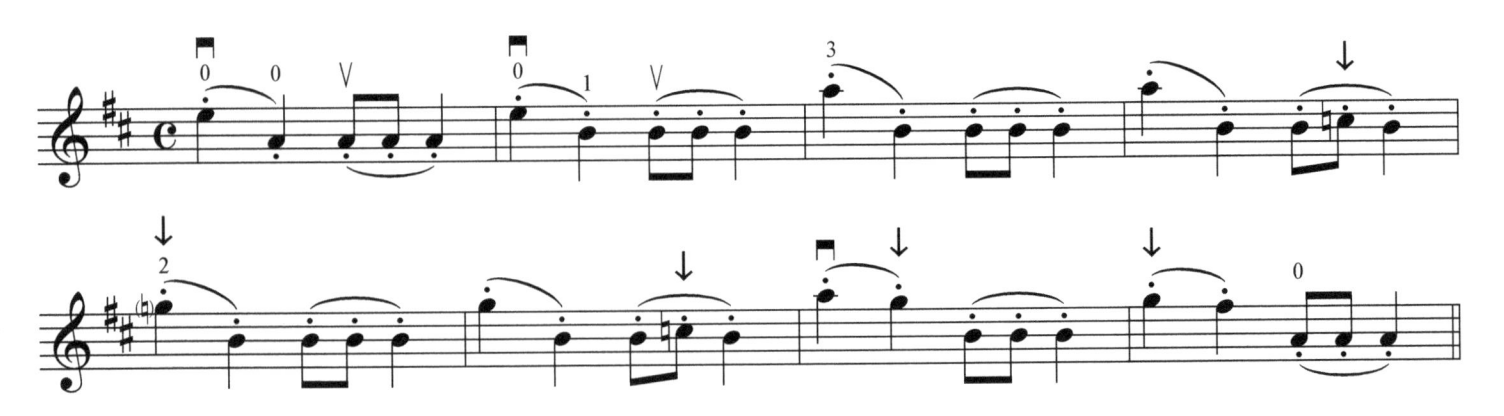

©2020 C. Harvey Publications   All Rights Reserved.

The Rieding Violin Concerto in B Minor - Preparatory Exercises for Movement Three

15. Agility: Measures 73-76

16. Rhythm and Fluency: Measures 73-76

The Rieding Violin Concerto in B Minor - Preparatory Exercises for Movement Three

17. Learning the Notes: Measures 79-80

18. String Crossing and Rhythm: Measures 83-84

©2020 C. Harvey Publications   All Rights Reserved.

The Rieding Violin Concerto in B Minor - Preparatory Exercises for Movement Three

19. Finger Spacing and Speed: Measures 87-90

20. Chord: Measure 91

©2020 C. Harvey Publications All Rights Reserved.

Movement Three With Study Notes

O. Rieding
Edited by C. Harvey

Allegro Moderato: Moderately (medium) lively or quick.

Study Tempo: ♩=44-84   Performance Tempo: ♩=88-132

©2020 C. Harvey Publications All Rights Reserved.

The Rieding Violin Concerto in B Minor - Movement Three With Study Notes

The Rieding Violin Concerto in B Minor - Movement Three With Study Notes

The Rieding Violin Concerto in B Minor - Movement Three With Study Notes

©2020 C. Harvey Publications All Rights Reserved.

Concerto in B Minor - Solo Part

O. Rieding, Op. 35

The Rieding Violin Concerto in B Minor - Movement One, Solo Part

The Rieding Violin Concerto in B Minor - Movement Two, Solo Part

This page is left blank for page turns.

The Rieding Violin Concerto in B Minor - Movement Three, Solo Part

Allegro Moderato

The Rieding Violin Concerto in B Minor - Movement Three, Solo Part

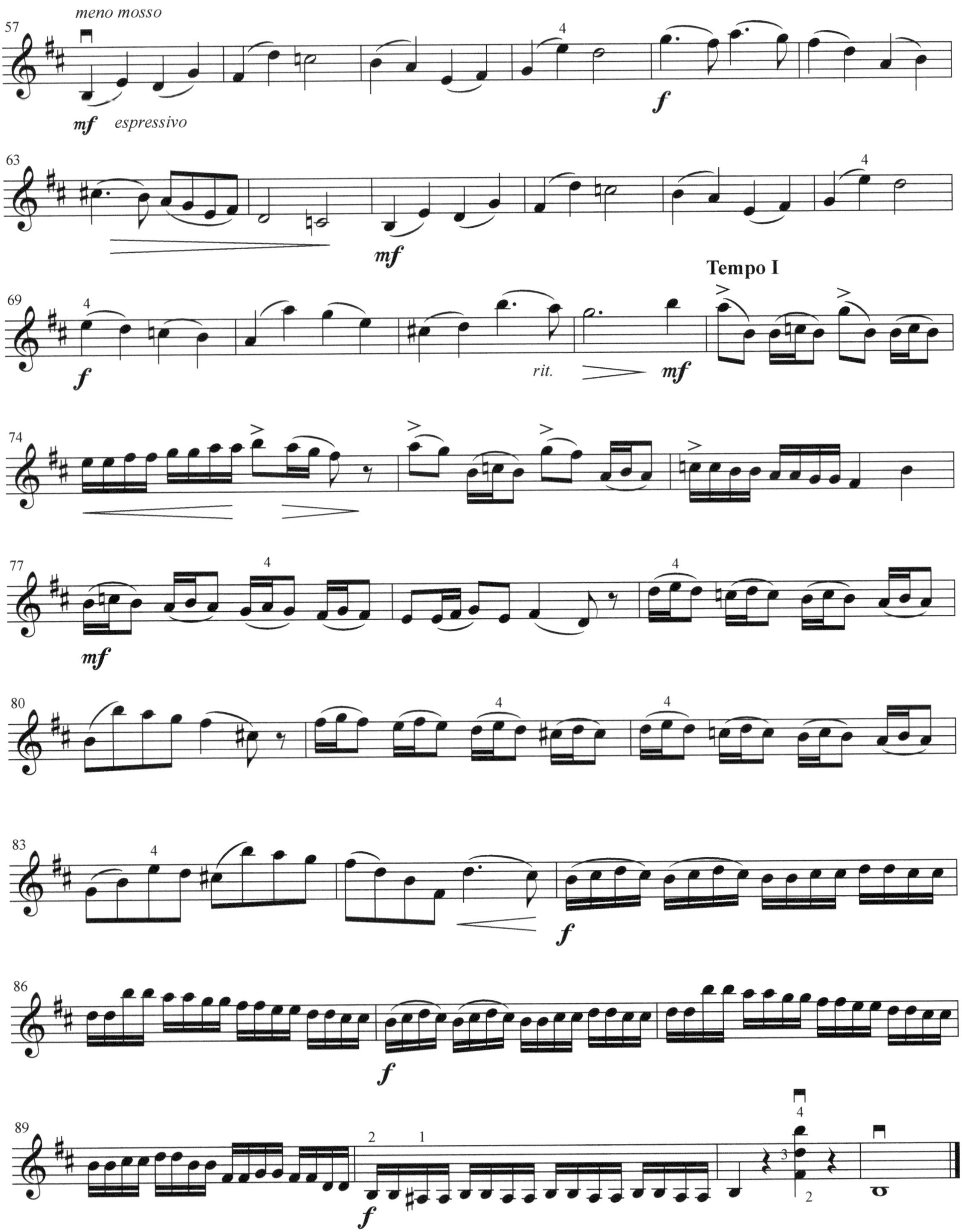
meno mosso
mf
espressivo
Tempo I
rit.

This page is left blank for page turns.

Concerto in B Minor - Duet

Concerto by O. Rieding
Duet by M. Harvey

Allegro Moderato

The Rieding Violin Concerto in B Minor - Movement One, Duet

The Rieding Violin Concerto in B Minor - Movement One, Duet

The Rieding Violin Concerto in B Minor - Movement One, Duet

This page is left blank for page turns.

The Rieding Violin Concerto in B Minor - Movement Two, Duet

The Rieding Violin Concerto in B Minor - Movement Two, Duet

The Rieding Violin Concerto in B Minor - Movement Two, Duet

The Rieding Violin Concerto in B Minor - Movement Three, Duet

Allegro Moderato

©2020 C. Harvey Publications All Rights Reserved.

The Rieding Violin Concerto in B Minor - Movement Three, Duet

64

The Rieding Violin Concerto in B Minor - Movement Three, Duet

©2020 C. Harvey Publications All Rights Reserved.

The Rieding Violin Concerto in B Minor - Movement Three, Duet

The Rieding Violin Concerto in B Minor - Movement Three, Duet

The Rieding Violin Concerto in B Minor - Movement Three, Duet

Concerto in B Minor - Violin II

Duet by M. Harvey

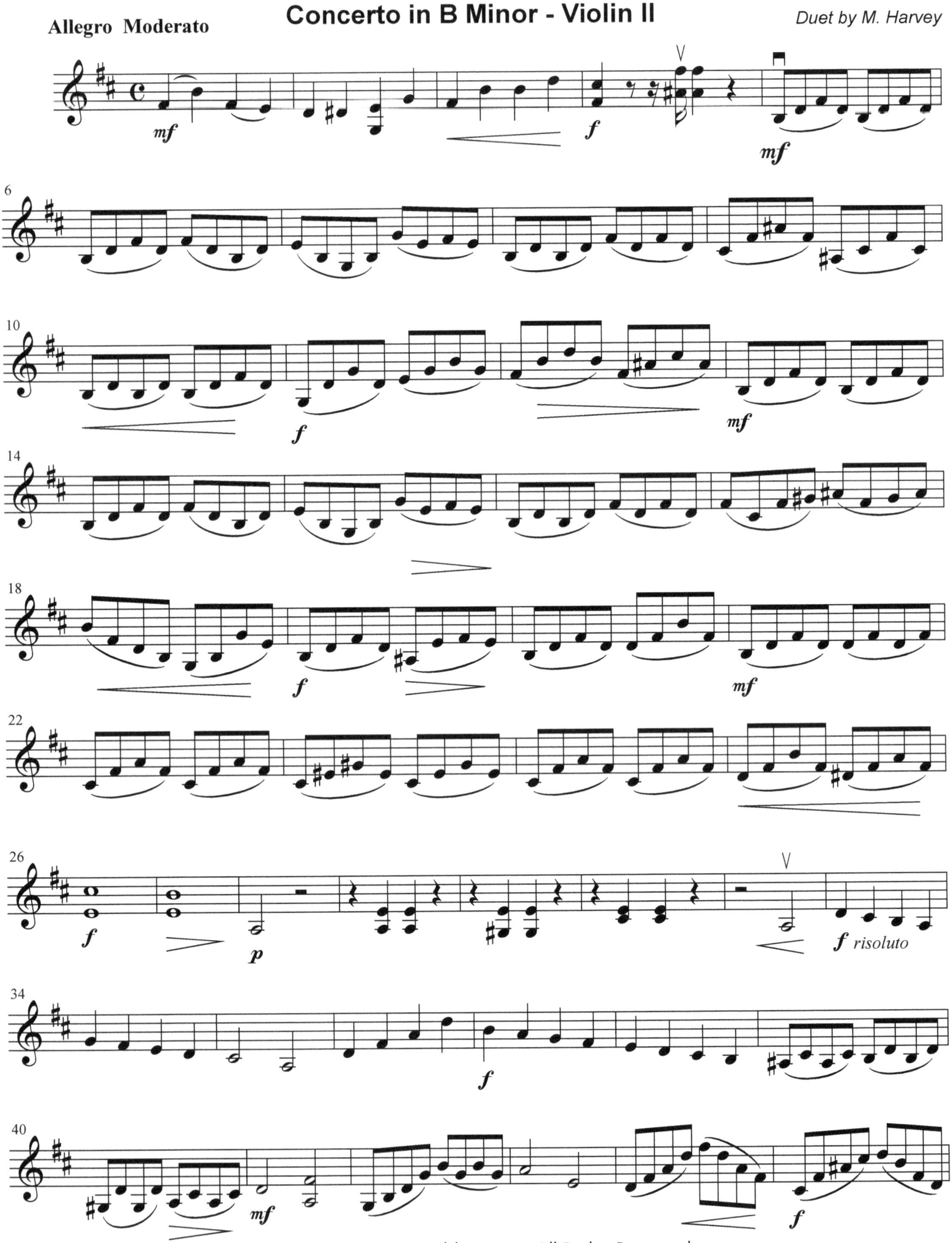

The Rieding Violin Concerto in B Minor - Movement One, Violin II

The Rieding Violin Concerto in B Minor - Movement Two, Violin II

The Rieding Violin Concerto in B Minor - Movement Two, Violin II

The Rieding Violin Concerto in B Minor - Movement Three, Violin II

The Rieding Violin Concerto in B Minor - Movement Three, Violin II

The Rieding Violin Concerto in B Minor - Movement Three, Violin II

Concerto in B Minor - Score

O. Rieding, Op. 35

76 — The Rieding Violin Concerto in B Minor - Movement One, Score

©2020 C. Harvey Publications   All Rights Reserved.

The Rieding Violin Concerto in B Minor - Movement One, Score

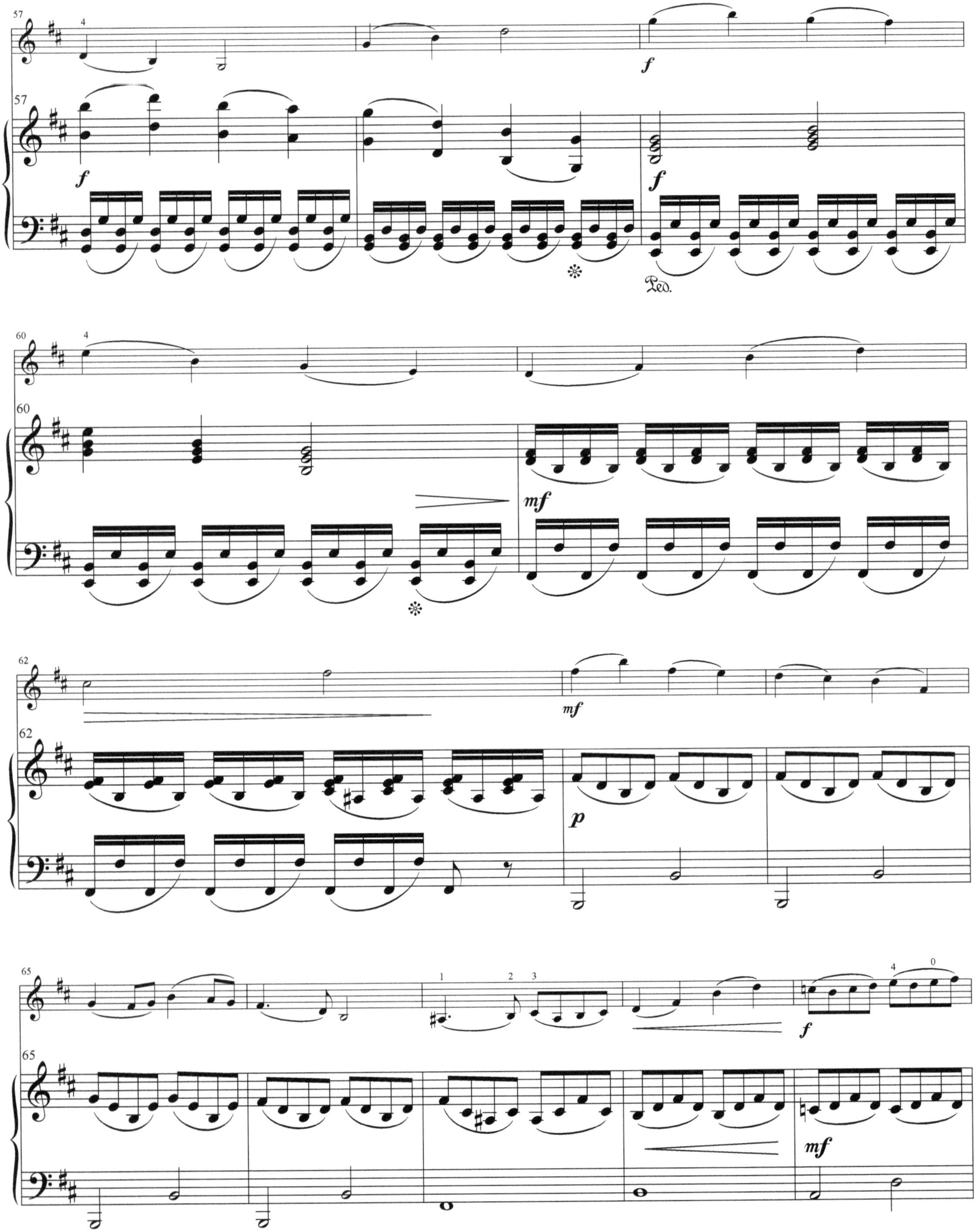
57
4
f
57
f
f
Ped.
60
4
60
mf
62
mf
62
p
65
1
2 3
4 0
f
65
mf

The Rieding Violin Concerto in B Minor - Movement One, Score

The Rieding Violin Concerto in B Minor - Movement Two, Score

The Rieding Violin Concerto in B Minor - Movement Two, Score

81

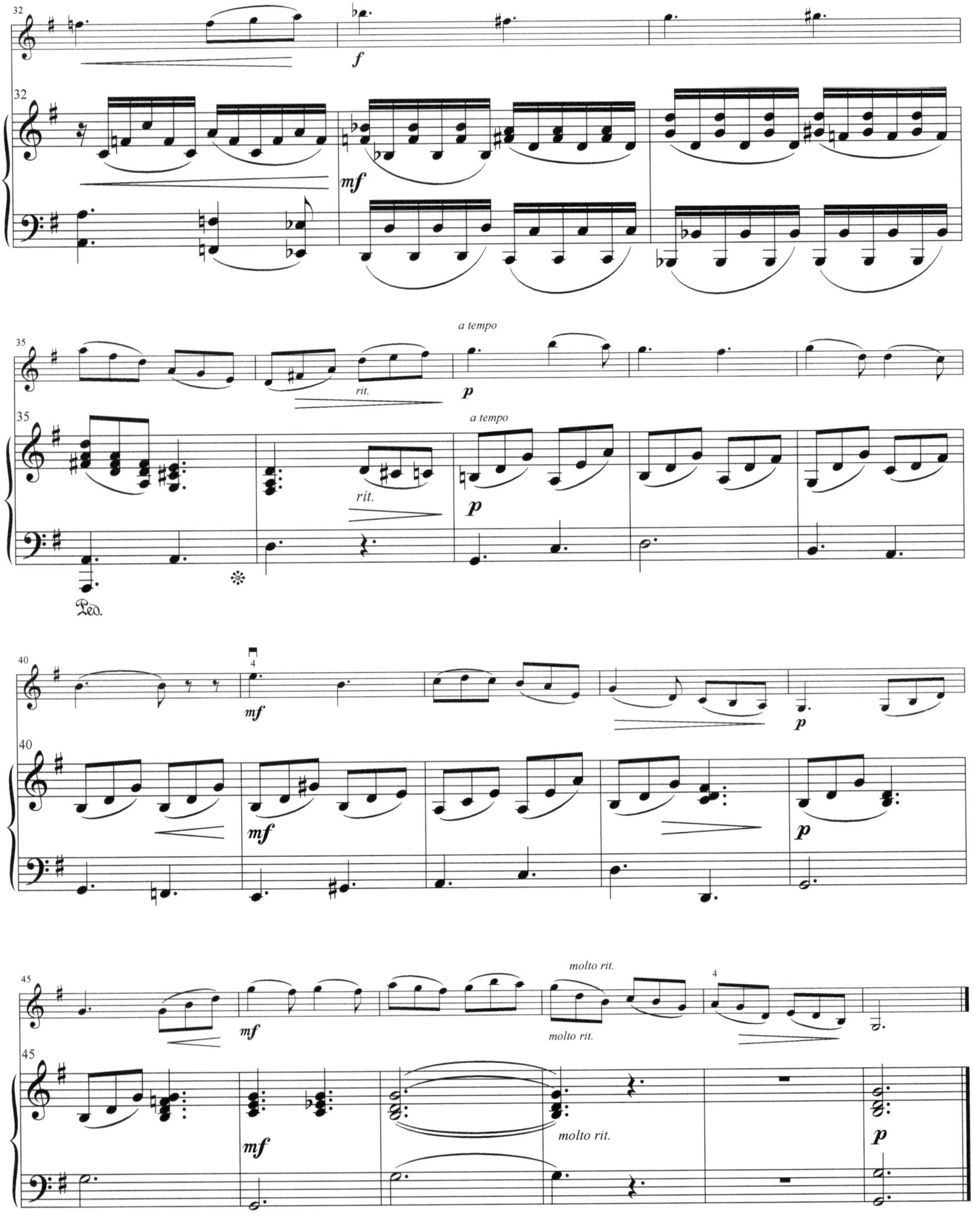
a tempo
rit.
a tempo
rit.
Ped.
molto rit.
molto rit.
molto rit.

The Rieding Violin Concerto in B Minor - Movement Three, Score

The Rieding Violin Concerto in B Minor - Movement Three, Score

The Rieding Violin Concerto in B Minor - Movement Three, Score

85

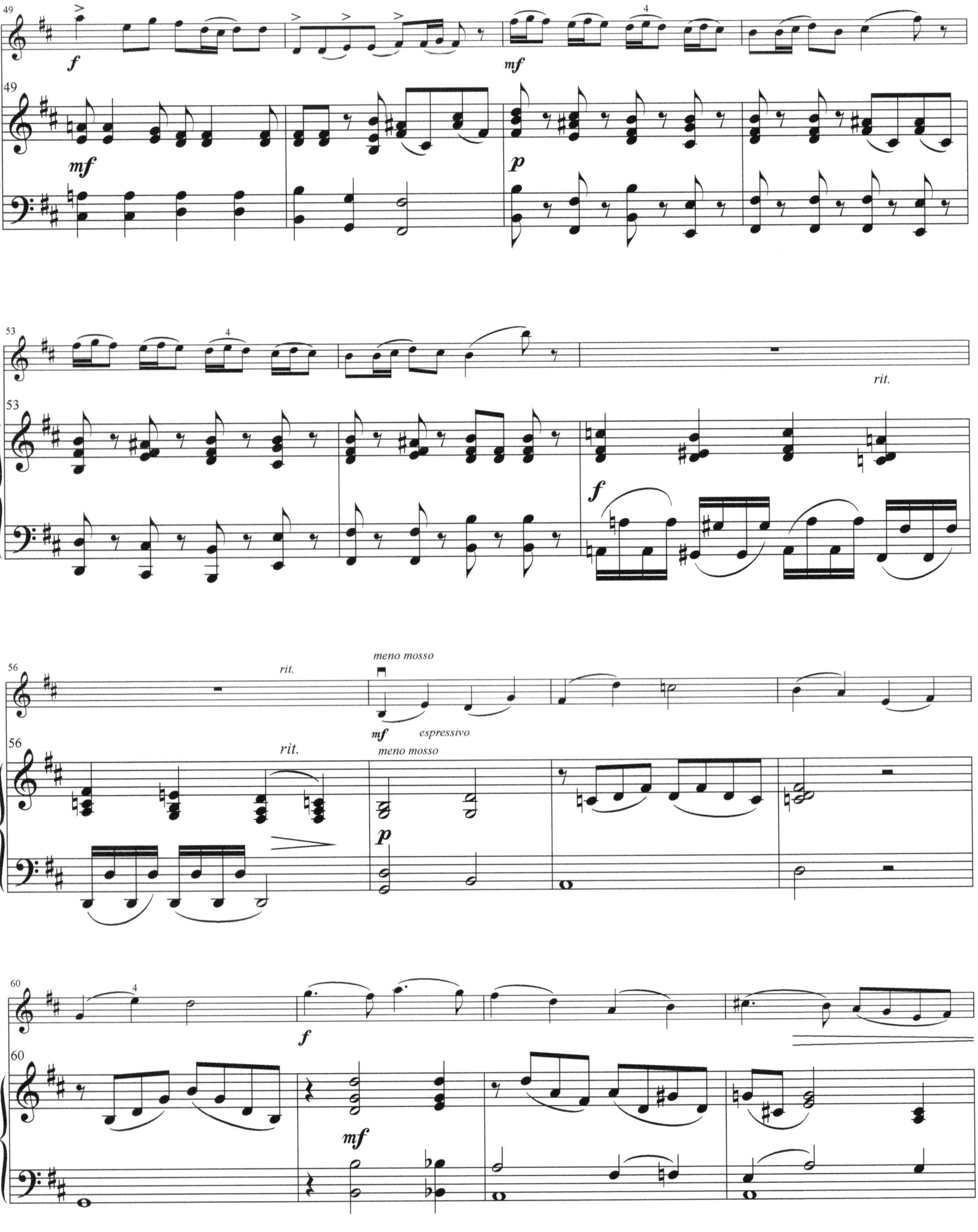
rit.
meno mosso
espressivo

The Rieding Violin Concerto in B Minor - Movement Three, Score

87

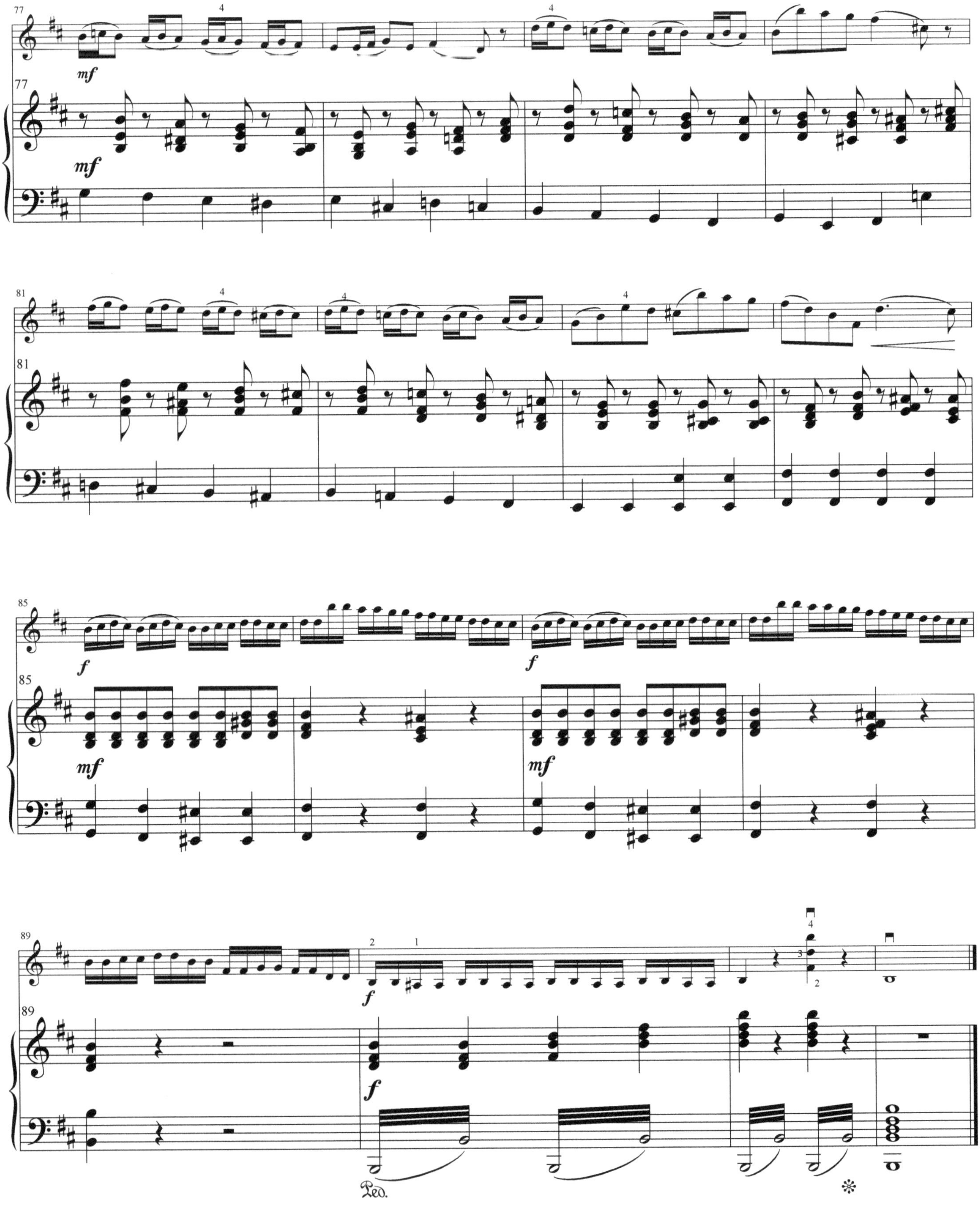
77
mf
77
mf
81
81
85
f
f
85
mf
mf
89
f
89
f
Ped.

Violin Curriculum Segments
When to Use the Rieding Concerto in a Course of Study

Step One: Beginning Level

Methods
- Learning the Violin, Books One (CHP280) and Two (CHP285)
- String Builder, Book One (published Belwin)
- Essential Elements for Violin, Book One or Essential Elements 2000 for Violin (published Hal Leonard)
- Suzuki Book One (if using a modified Suzuki approach) (published Summy-Birchard)

Exercises
- The Open-String Book for Violin (CHP249)
- Early Exercises for Violin (CHP183)
- The A-String Book for Violin (CHP213) and The D-String Book for Violin (CHP240)
- Knowing the Notes for Violin (CHP132)
- I Can Read Music, by Martin (published Summy-Birchard)

Supplements and Etudes
- Playing the Violin, Book One (CHP298)
- Beginning Fiddle Duets for Two Violins (CHP303)

Repertoire Books
- Stepping Stones for Violin (published Boosey & Hawkes)
- Waggon Wheels for Violin (published Boosey & Hawkes)
- Easy Solos for Beginning Violin (published Mel Bay)
- The Student Violinist: Bach (published Mel Bay)
- Violin Recital Album, First Position, Volume 1, by Sassmannshaus (published Bärenreiter)

Concertos/Concertinos
- Kuchler Concertino in G Major, Op. 11 (published Bosworth)

Note: Books published by C. Harvey Publications are noted with an item number (CHP101) and are available at www.charveypublications.com and/or www.learnstrings.com, as well as where you purchased this book.

©2020 C. Harvey Publications All Rights Reserved.

Step Two: Early-Intermediate Level; More Complicated First Position

Methods
- Playing in Keys for Violin (CHP254)
- String Builder for Violin, Book Two (published Belwin)
- Essential Elements for Violin, Book Two (published Hal Leonard)
- Suzuki Books Two and Three (if using a modified Suzuki approach) (published Summy-Birchard)

Exercises
- Finger Exercises for Violin, Book One (CHP185)
- The Triplet Book for Violin, Book One (CHP267)
- First Position Scale Studies for the Violin (CHP317)
- Scales in First Position for Violin by Whistler (published Rubank)
- Double Stop Beginnings for Violin, Book One (CHP247)
- Open-String Bow Workouts for Violin, Book One (CHP352)

Supplements and Etudes
- Playing the Violin, Book Two (CHP324)
- First Etude Album for Violin, by Whistler/Hummel (published Rubank)
- 60 Studies, Op. 45, Book One, by Wohlfahrt (published Schirmer or Carl Fischer)
- Flying Fiddle Duets for Two Violins, Book One (CHP263) and Book Two (CHP307)

Repertoire Books and Solo Pieces
- Solo Time for Strings, Book Three, by Etling (published Alfred)
- Solos for Young Violinists, Book One, by Barber (first half of book) (published Alfred)
- Violin Recital Album, First Position, Volume 2, by Sassmannshaus (published Baerenreiter)
- Kreisler *Chanson Louis VIII & Pavane* (published Carl Fischer)

Concertos/Concertinos (in approximate order of study)
- **Rieding Concerto in B Minor, Op. 35 (this piece)**
- Seitz Concerto No. 2 (published Bosworth or Schirmer)
- Seitz Concerto No. 5 (published Bosworth or Schirmer)

Note: Books published by C. Harvey Publications are noted with an item number (CHP101) and are available at www.charveypublications.com and/or www.learnstrings.com, as well as where you purchased this book.

©2020 C. Harvey Publications   All Rights Reserved.

Step Three: Intermediate Level; Starting Third Position

Methods
- Third Position for the Violin (CHP196)
- Suzuki Books Three, Four (if using a modified Suzuki approach) (published Summy-Birchard)
- Introducing the Positions, Vol. One, by Whistler (published Rubank)

Exercises
- Finger Exercises for Violin, Book Two (first position) (CHP266)
- Double Stop Beginnings for Violin, Book Two (first position) (CHP248)
- Third Position Study Book for the Violin (CHP217)
- The Two Octaves Book for Violin (CHP265)

Supplements and Etudes
- 60 Studies, Op. 45, Book Two, by Wohlfahrt (published Schirmer or Carl Fischer)

Repertoire Books
- Solo Time for Strings, Book Four, by Etling (published Alfred)
- Solos for Young Violinists, Book One, by Barber (last half of book) (published Alfred)

Short Pieces
- Gabriel-Marie *La Cinquantaine* (published Carl Fischer)
- Fiocco *Allegro* (published International or Schott)
- Portnoff *Russian Fantasia* (published Carl Fischer)

Concertos/Concertinos (in approximate order of study)
- Kuchler Concertino in D Major, Op. 15 (published Bosworth)
- Ruegger Concertante in G Major (published Carl Fischer)
- Vivaldi Concerto in G Major, RV310m, Op. 3, no. 3 (published Schott or Edition Hug)

Note: Books published by C. Harvey Publications are noted with an item number (CHP101) and are available at www.charveypublications.com and/or www.learnstrings.com, as well as where you purchased this book.

©2020 C. Harvey Publications All Rights Reserved.

Step Four: Late-Intermediate Level; Learning Other Positions

Methods
- Second Position for the Violin (CHP253)
- Fourth Position for the Violin (CHP246)
- Suzuki Book Five (if using a modified Suzuki approach) (published Summy-Birchard)
- Introducing the Positions, Vol. Two, by Whistler (published Rubank)

Exercises
- G Major Shifting for the Violin (CHP257)
- Serial Shifting for the Violin (CHP195)
- Octaves for the Violin, Book One (CHP166)
- Scale Studies (One String) for the Violin, Part One (CHP178)
- Three-Octave Scales for the Violin (CHP354)
- Shifting in Keys for Violin (CHP256)

Supplements and Etudes
- Classical Syncs: Duets for Two Violins (CHP320)
- 6 Canonic Sonatas for Two Violins, by Telemann (published International)
- Six Petits Duos, Op. 48 by Pleyel (published Schirmer)
- Etudes Speciales, Op. 36, Book 1, by Mazas (published Schirmer)
- 42 Studies for Violin, by Kreutzer (published Schirmer, International, and others)

Short Pieces
- Kreisler *Sicilienne and Rigaudon* (published Carl Fischer)
- Solos for Young Violinists, Book Two, by Barber (published Alfred)
- Solos for the Violin Player by Gingold (published Schirmer)

Sonatas/Concertos (in approximate order of study)
- Vivaldi Concerto in A Minor, Op. 3, No. 6 (published International)
- Rieding Concertino in A Minor, Op. 21 (published Bosworth)
- Handel Sonatas No. 3, 4 (published Schirmer or Carl Fischer)
- The Bach Double Violin Concerto Study Book, Vol. One (CHP342)
- Bach Concerto in A Minor (published Schirmer, International, and others)

Note: Books published by C. Harvey Publications are noted with an item number (CHP101) and are available at www.charveypublications.com and/or www.learnstrings.com, as well as where you purchased this book.

Also Available from C. Harvey Publications

The Bach Double Violin Concerto Study Book, Vol. 1
CHP342

- Exercises are included to teach you every measure.
- Essential violin technique is distilled and presented.
- The complete violin parts to the Concerto are included.
- Master this quintessential violin piece!

www.charveypublications.com - print books
www.learnstrings.com - downloadable books

©2020 C. Harvey Publications   All Rights Reserved.